Delicious Desserts

Stunning Peanut Butter-Chocolate Layer Cake

Prep: 20 min. | Total: 1 hr 15 min. (incl. cooling) | Makes: 16 servings.

What you need

- 1 pkg. (2-layer size) yellow cake mix
- 2 pkg. (3.4 oz. each) **JELL-O** Vanilla Flavor Instant Pudding, divided
- 1 cup cold milk
- ½ cup **PLANTERS** Creamy Peanut Butter
- 6 oz. **BAKER'S** Semi-Sweet Chocolate, divided
- 1 pkg. (8 oz.) **PHILADELPHIA** Cream Cheese, cubed, softened
- ¼ cup butter, cut up, softened
- 3 cups powdered sugar
- ½ cup **PLANTERS** Lightly Salted Dry Roasted Peanuts, chopped

Make It

HEAT oven to 350°F.

LINE 13×9-inch pan with foil, with ends of foil extending over sides; spray with cooking spray. Prepare cake batter as directed on package, adding 1 pkg. dry pudding mix; beat 2 min. Pour into prepared pan. Bake 25 min. or until toothpick inserted in center comes out clean. Cool completely.

MEANWHILE, prepare filling and frosting. For filling, beat remaining dry pudding mix and milk in medium bowl with whisk 2 min. Stir in peanut butter until blended. For frosting, microwave 3 oz. chocolate in large microwaveable bowl on HIGH 1 min. or until melted, stirring after 30 sec. Add cream cheese and butter; beat with mixer until blended. Gradually beat in sugar. Use remaining chocolate to make chocolate curls as directed in How-To tip on page 24.

USE foil handles to lift cake from pan; cut crosswise in half. Place 1 cake half, top-side down, on plate; spread with peanut butter filling. Cover with remaining cake half, top-side up. Spread top and sides with chocolate frosting. Press nuts halfway up sides of cake; top with chocolate curls.

Boston Cream Cheesecake

Prep: 35 min. | Total: 5 hr 20 min. (incl. refrigerating) | Makes: 16 servings.

What you need

- 1 pkg. (1-layer size) yellow cake mix
- 3 pkg. (8 oz. each) **PHILADELPHIA** Cream Cheese, softened
- ¾ cup granulated sugar
- 2 tsp. vanilla, divided
- ¾ cup **BREAKSTONE'S** or **KNUDSEN** Sour Cream
- 3 eggs
- 2 oz. **BAKER'S** Unsweetened Chocolate
- 3 Tbsp. milk
- 2 Tbsp. butter or margarine
- 1 cup powdered sugar

Make It

HEAT oven to 325°F.

GREASE bottom of 9-inch springform pan. Prepare cake mix as directed on package; pour into prepared pan. Bake 25 min. if using silver springform pan. (Bake at 300°F for 20 min. if using a dark nonstick springform pan.) Cool.

BEAT cream cheese, granulated sugar and 1 tsp. of the vanilla in large bowl with electric mixer on medium speed until well blended. Add sour cream; mix well. Add eggs, 1 at a time, mixing on low speed after each addition just until blended. Pour over cake layer in pan.

BAKE 40 to 45 min. or until center is almost set if using a silver springform pan. (Bake at 300°F for 40 to 45 min. if using a dark nonstick springform pan.) Run knife or metal spatula around rim of pan to loosen cake; cool before removing rim of pan.

PLACE chocolate, milk and butter in medium microwaveable bowl. Microwave on HIGH 2 min. or until butter is melted, stirring after 1 min. Stir until chocolate is completely melted. Add powdered sugar and remaining 1 tsp. vanilla; mix well. Spread over cooled cheesecake. Refrigerate 4 hours or overnight.

Chocolate Cluster-Peanut Butter Cake

Prep: 20 min. | Total: 1 hr 20 min. (incl. cooling) | Makes: 16 servings.

What you need

- 1 pkg. (2-layer size) chocolate cake mix
- 1 pkg. (3.4 oz.) **JELL-O** Vanilla Flavor Instant Pudding
- 1 cup cold milk
- ½ cup **PLANTERS** Creamy Peanut Butter
- ½ cup **PLANTERS** Dry Roasted Peanuts
- 2 oz. **BAKER'S** Semi-Sweet Chocolate, melted
- 1½ cups thawed **COOL WHIP** Whipped Topping

Make It

HEAT oven to 350°F.

PREPARE cake batter and bake as directed on package for 2 (9-inch) round cake layers. Cool in pans 10 min.; remove to wire racks. Cool completely. Meanwhile, beat dry pudding mix and milk with whisk 2 min. Add peanut butter; mix well. Refrigerate until ready to use.

MIX nuts and melted chocolate until nuts are evenly coated. Drop by tablespoonfuls onto waxed paper-covered baking sheet. Refrigerate 10 min. or until firm.

STACK cake layers on plate, filling with 1 cup pudding mixture. Gently stir COOL WHIP into remaining pudding mixture. Spread over top and side of cake. Decorate with chocolate-nut clusters.

JELL-O Cookie Gems

Prep: 20 min. | Total: 1 hr 1 min. (incl. refrigerating) | Makes: 30 servings, 2 cookies each.

What you need

1 pkg. (8 oz.) **PHILADELPHIA** Cream Cheese, softened

¾ cup butter, softened

1 cup granulated sugar

2 tsp. vanilla

2¼ cups flour

1 pkg. (3 oz.) **JELL-O** Raspberry Flavor Gelatin

½ tsp. baking soda

2 Tbsp. powdered sugar

Make It

BEAT first 4 ingredients in large bowl with mixer until blended. Mix flour, dry gelatin mix and baking soda; gradually add to cream cheese mixture, mixing well after each addition. Refrigerate 30 min.

HEAT oven to 375°F. Roll dough into 60 (1-inch) balls. Place, 2 inches apart, on baking sheets sprayed with cooking spray.

BAKE 9 to 11 min. or until edges are lightly browned. Cool on baking sheets 2 min. Remove to wire racks; cool completely.

SPRINKLE with powdered sugar just before serving.

VARIATION
Prepare using JELL-O Lime Flavor Gelatin.

BAKER'S ONE BOWL
Million Dollar Fudge

Prep: 25 min. | Total: 25 min. | Makes: 60 servings, 1 piece each.

What you need

½ cup butter or margarine

4½ cups sugar

1 can (12 oz.) evaporated milk

3 pkg. (12 oz. each) **BAKER'S** Semi-Sweet Chocolate Chunks

1 jar (7 oz.) **JET-PUFFED** Marshmallow Creme

3 cups **PLANTERS** Chopped Pecans

1 tsp. salt

1 tsp. vanilla

Make It

BRING butter, sugar and milk to full rolling boil in large saucepan on medium heat, stirring constantly. Boil an additional 5 min., stirring constantly.

REMOVE from heat. Gradually add chocolate chunks, stirring until chocolate is completely melted after each addition. Add remaining ingredients; mix well.

POUR into 15×10×1-inch pan sprayed with cooking spray. Cool completely.

To make Rocky Road Fudge, prepare as directed, stirring 2 cups JET-PUFFED Miniature Marshmallows into the hot fudge mixture before pouring into pan.

Snow-Covered Almond Crescents

Prep: 20 min. | Total: 1 hr 12 min. (incl. refrigerating) | Makes: 5 doz. or 30 servings, 2 cookies each.

What you need

- 1 pkg. (8 oz.) **PHILADELPHIA** Cream Cheese, softened
- ¾ cup butter, softened
- 1 cup granulated sugar
- 2 tsp. vanilla
- ½ tsp. almond extract
- 2¼ cups flour
- ½ tsp. baking soda
- 1 cup finely chopped **PLANTERS** Slivered Almonds
- ¾ cup powdered sugar

Make It

BEAT first 5 ingredients in large bowl with mixer until well blended. Add flour and baking soda; mix well. Stir in nuts. Refrigerate 30 min.

HEAT oven to 350°F. Roll dough into 60 (1-inch) balls; shape each into crescent shape. Place, 2 inches apart, on baking sheets. Flatten slightly.

BAKE 10 to 12 min. or until lightly browned. Cool 3 min. on baking sheets; transfer to wire racks. Cool completely. Sprinkle with powdered sugar.

Chocolate Sugar Cookies

Prep: 20 min. | Total: 45 min. (incl. refrigerating) | Makes: about 3½ doz. or 21 servings, 2 cookies each.

What you need

     2 cups flour

     1 tsp. baking soda

    ¼ tsp. salt

     4 oz. **BAKER'S** Unsweetened Chocolate

     1 cup butter or margarine

  1½ cups sugar, divided

     1 egg

     1 tsp. vanilla

Make It

MIX flour, baking soda and salt; set aside. Microwave chocolate and butter in large microwaveable bowl on HIGH 2 min. or until butter is melted. Stir until chocolate is completely melted. Add 1 cup sugar, egg and vanilla; mix well. Stir in flour mixture until well blended. Refrigerate 15 min. or until dough is easy to handle.

HEAT oven to 375°F. Shape dough into 1-inch balls; roll in remaining sugar. Place, 2 inches apart, on baking sheets.

BAKE 8 to 10 min. or until centers are set. Cool on baking sheets 1 min. Remove to wire racks; cool completely.

CHOCOLATE-CARAMEL SUGAR COOKIES
Omit ½ cup of the sugar. Prepare dough and shape into balls as directed. Roll in ½ cup chopped PLANTERS Pecans instead of the sugar. Place, 2 inches apart, on baking sheets. Make indentation in each ball. Bake as directed. Microwave 1 pkg. (14 oz.) KRAFT Caramels and 2 Tbsp. milk in microwaveable bowl on HIGH 3 min. or until caramels are completely melted, stirring after 2 min. Spoon into centers of cookies. Drizzle with melted BAKER'S Semi-Sweet Chocolate. Cool completely.

Tuxedo Cake

Prep: 30 min. | Total: 1 hr 43 min. (incl. cooling) | Makes: 16 servings.

What you need

- 1 pkg. (2-layer size) devil's food cake mix
- 1 pkg. (3.9 oz.) **JELL-O** Chocolate Instant Pudding
- 1½ pkg. (8 oz. each) **PHILADELPHIA** Cream Cheese, softened
- ½ cup butter, softened
- 1½ tsp. vanilla
- 6 cups powdered sugar
- ½ of 8-oz. tub **COOL WHIP** Whipped Topping (Do not thaw.)
- 2 oz. **BAKER'S** Semi-Sweet Chocolate

  Chocolate Curls (see How-To tip, page 24)

Make It

HEAT oven to 350°F.

PREPARE cake batter and bake as directed on package for 2 (9-inch) round cake layers, blending dry pudding mix into batter before pouring into prepared pans. Cool 10 min. Loosen cakes from sides of pans with knife. Invert onto wire racks; gently remove pans. Cool cakes completely.

MEANWHILE, beat cream cheese, butter and vanilla in large bowl with mixer until blended. Gradually beat in sugar.

CUT each cake layer horizontally in half. Stack on plate, spreading ¾ cup cream cheese frosting between each layer. Spread remaining frosting onto top and sides of cake.

MICROWAVE COOL WHIP and chocolate in microwaveable bowl on HIGH 1½ min., stirring after 1 min.; stir until chocolate is completely melted and mixture is well blended. Cool 5 min. Pour over cake, letting excess drip down sides. Store cake in refrigerator. Garnish with Chocolate Curls before serving.

Chocolate Bliss–
Caramel Brownies

Prep: 20 min. | Total: 55 min. | Makes: 36 servings.

What you need

- 4 oz. **BAKER'S** Unsweetened Chocolate
- ¾ cup butter or margarine
- 2 cups sugar
- 4 eggs
- 1 cup flour
- 1 cup chopped **PLANTERS** Pecans or Walnuts
- 25 **KRAFT** Caramels
- 2 Tbsp. milk
- 1 pkg. (12 oz.) **BAKER'S** Semi-Sweet Chocolate Chunks

Make It

HEAT oven to 350°F.

LINE 13×9-inch baking pan with foil, with ends extending over sides of pan. Spray with cooking spray.

MICROWAVE unsweetened chocolate and butter in large microwaveable bowl on HIGH 2 min. or until butter is melted. Stir until chocolate is completely melted. Add sugar; mix well. Blend in eggs. Add flour; mix well. Stir in nuts. Spread into prepared pan.

BAKE 30 to 35 min. or until toothpick inserted in center comes out with fudgy crumbs. (Do not overbake.) Meanwhile, microwave caramels and milk in microwaveable bowl on HIGH 2½ min., stirring after 1 min. Stir until caramels are completely melted and mixture is well blended.

SPREAD caramel sauce over brownie; cool 5 min. Sprinkle with chocolate chunks. Cool completely. Use foil handles to lift brownies from pan before cutting to serve.

BAKER'S ONE BOWL
Midnight Bliss Cake

Prep: 15 min. | Total: 2 hr 15 min. (incl. cooling) | Makes: 18 servings.

What you need

- 4 eggs
- 1 pkg. (2-layer size) chocolate cake mix, any variety
- 1 container (8 oz.) **BREAKSTONE'S** or **KNUDSEN** Sour Cream
- 1 pkg. (3.9 oz.) **JELL-O** Chocolate Instant Pudding
- ½ cup oil
- ½ cup water
- ½ cup **MAXWELL HOUSE INTERNATIONAL CAFÉ**, any café flavor
- 8 oz. **BAKER'S** Semi-Sweet Chocolate, chopped
- 2 Tbsp. powdered sugar

Make It

HEAT oven to 350°F.

BEAT all ingredients except coffee granules, chopped chocolate and powdered sugar in large bowl with mixer until well blended. Stir in coffee granules and chopped chocolate.

POUR into 12-cup fluted tube pan or 10-inch tube pan sprayed with cooking spray.

BAKE 50 min. to 1 hour or until toothpick inserted near center comes out clean. Cool cake in pan 10 min. Loosen cake from side of pan with knife. Invert cake onto wire rack; gently remove pan. Cool completely. Transfer to plate just before serving; sprinkle with powdered sugar.

Substitute 2 Tbsp. MAXWELL HOUSE Instant Coffee for the 1/2 cup MAXWELL HOUSE INTERNATIONAL CAFÉ.

Chocolate-Banana Heaven Cake

Prep: 20 min. | Total: 1 hr 35 min. (incl. cooling) | Makes: 16 servings.

What you need

1 pkg. (2-layer size) chocolate cake mix (not pudding in the mix variety)

½ cup unsweetened cocoa powder

1 cup prepared **MAXWELL HOUSE** Instant Coffee, cooled

4 fully ripe bananas, mashed

3 eggs

⅓ cup water

1 tsp. **MAXWELL HOUSE** Instant Coffee

2 Tbsp. milk, warmed

1 pkg. (8 oz.) **PHILADELPHIA** Cream Cheese, softened

3 oz. **BAKER'S** Semi-Sweet Chocolate, melted

2 cups powdered sugar

½ cup **PLANTERS** Chopped Pecans

Chocolate Curls (optional)

Make It

HEAT oven to 350°F. Grease and flour 2 (9-inch) round cake pans. Cover bottoms of pans with waxed paper; set aside.

COMBINE cake mix and cocoa powder in large bowl. Add the prepared coffee, bananas, eggs and water; beat with electric mixer on low speed 30 sec., stopping frequently to scrape bottom and side of bowl. Beat on medium speed 2 min.; pour evenly into prepared pans.

BAKE 30 to 35 min. or until toothpick inserted in centers comes out clean. Cool 10 min.; remove from pans to wire racks. Immediately remove waxed paper. Cool cake layers completely.

DISSOLVE 1 tsp. instant coffee in the warm milk. Beat cream cheese with electric mixer on medium speed until creamy. Add milk mixture; beat 2 min. Blend in melted chocolate. Add sugar; beat until light and fluffy. Use to fill and frost cooled cake layers. Immediately press nuts into frosting on side of cake. Garnish with Chocolate Curls, if desired.

HOW TO MAKE CHOCOLATE CURLS
Microwave 3 oz. BAKER'S Semi-Sweet or White Chocolate and ½ tsp. shortening in microwaveable bowl on HIGH 30 sec.; stir. Microwave 30 to 40 sec. or until chocolate is almost melted; stir until completely melted. Spread into thin layer on baking sheet. Refrigerate 10 min. or until firm, but still pliable. Push metal spatula firmly across baking sheet, under the chocolate, to make curls. (If chocolate is too firm, let stand a few minutes at room temperature; refrigerate again if it becomes too soft.)

VARIATION
Prepare as directed, substituting muffin pans for the round cake pans. Spoon batter evenly into 24 paper-lined medium muffin cups, filling each cup two-thirds full. Bake at 350°F for 25 to 30 min. or until wooden toothpick inserted in centers comes out clean. Cool completely on wire racks before spreading with frosting. Makes 2 doz. or 24 servings, 1 cupcake each.

Italian-Style Crème Brûlée

Prep: 15 min. | Total: 30 min. (incl. refrigerating) | Makes: 8 servings, ½ cup each.

What you need

2 pkg. (3.4 oz. each) **JELL-O** Vanilla Flavor Instant Pudding

1½ cups cold milk

1 cup cold half-and-half

½ cup Marsala wine

¼ cup packed brown sugar

1 Tbsp. powdered sugar

1 cup mixed fresh berries (blueberries, raspberries, blackberries)

Make It

BEAT dry pudding mixes, milk, half-and-half and wine with whisk 2 min.

POUR into shallow 1-qt. baking dish. Refrigerate 15 min.

HEAT broiler. Mix sugars; sprinkle over pudding. Broil, 6 inches from heat, 3 to 5 min. or until sugars are melted and caramelized. Let stand 5 min. Top with fruit. Serve immediately.

SUBSTITUTE
Substitute Madeira wine or additional milk for the Marsala wine.

Mile-High Peanut Butter Pie

Prep: 15 min. | Total: 3 hr 40 min. (incl. refrigerating) | Makes: 12 servings.

What you need

35 **NILLA** Wafers, finely crushed (about 1 cup)

¼ cup butter, melted

1 pkg. (3.9 oz.) **JELL-O** Chocolate Instant Pudding

2 cups cold milk, divided

4 oz. (½ of 8-oz. pkg.) **PHILADELPHIA** Cream Cheese, softened

1 pkg. (3.4 oz.) **JELL-O** Vanilla Flavor Instant Pudding

½ cup **PLANTERS** Creamy Peanut Butter, divided

2 cups thawed **COOL WHIP** Whipped Topping, divided

½ oz. **BAKER'S** Semi-Sweet Chocolate

Make It

HEAT oven to 375°F.

MIX wafer crumbs and butter until well blended; press onto bottom and up side of 9-inch pie plate. Bake 10 min.; cool.

BEAT dry chocolate pudding mix and 1 cup milk with whisk 2 min. (Pudding will be thick.) Spread onto bottom of crust. Gradually add remaining milk to cream cheese in large bowl, beating with mixer until mixture is well blended. Add dry vanilla pudding mix; beat 2 min. Reserve 1 Tbsp. peanut butter. Add remaining peanut butter to vanilla pudding mixture; beat until well blended. Stir in 1 cup COOL WHIP. Spread over chocolate pudding layer to within 1 inch of edge. Top with remaining COOL WHIP.

REFRIGERATE 3 hours. When ready to serve, microwave remaining peanut butter in microwaveable bowl on HIGH 15 sec. or until melted. Melt chocolate as directed on package. Drizzle chocolate, then peanut butter over pie.

Kansas City Mud Pie

Prep: 1 hr | Total: 4 hr (incl. refrigerating) | Makes: 16 servings.

What you need

1¼ cups finely chopped **PLANTERS** Pecans

¾ cup flour

¼ cup butter or margarine, melted

2 pkg. (8 oz. each) **PHILADELPHIA** Cream Cheese, softened

1½ cups sifted powdered sugar

1 tub (8 oz.) **COOL WHIP** Whipped Topping, thawed, divided

2 pkg. (3.9 oz. each) **JELL-O** Chocolate Instant Pudding

2⅔ cups cold milk

Make It

HEAT oven to 375°F.

MIX nuts, flour and butter; press onto bottom of 9-inch springform pan. Bake 20 min. Cool.

BEAT cream cheese and sugar with mixer until well blended. Gently stir in 1½ cups COOL WHIP; spread over crust. Beat dry pudding mixes and milk with whisk 2 min. or until well blended. Spoon over cream cheese layer.

REFRIGERATE several hours or until firm. Run knife or metal spatula around rim of pan to loosen pie; remove rim. Garnish pie with remaining COOL WHIP just before serving.

Drizzle each serving plate with 1 Tbsp. raspberry sauce before topping with pie slice.